A Bug's World

Buzz with the Bees

By Karen Latchana Kenney
Illustrated by Lisa Hedicker

Content Consultant
Clyde Sorenson, PhD
Professor of Entomology
North Carolina State University

magic Wagon

visit us at www.abdopublishing.com

Published by Magic Wagon, a division of the ABDO Group, 8000 West 78th Street, Edina, Minnesota 55439.
Copyright © 2011 by Abdo Consulting Group, Inc. International copyrights reserved in all countries. All rights
reserved. No part of this book may be reproduced in any form without written permission from the publisher.

Looking Glass Library™ is a trademark and logo of Magic Wagon.

Printed in the United States of America, North Mankato, Minnesota.
042010
092010

Text by Karen Latchana Kenney
Illustrations by Lisa Hedicker
Edited by Amy Van Zee
Interior layout and design by Becky Daum
Cover design by Craig Hinton

Library of Congress Cataloging-in-Publication Data
Kenney, Karen Latchana.
 Buzz with the bees / by Karen Latchana Kenney ; illustrated by Lisa Hedicker.
    p. cm. — (A bug's world)
 Includes index.
 ISBN 978-1-60270-784-9
 1. Bees—Juvenile literature. I. Hedicker, Lisa, 1984– , ill. II. Title.
 QL565.2.K46 2011
 595.79'9—dc22
                              2009052903

Table of Contents

Busy Bees

Buzz, buzz, buzz. Bees flit from flower to flower. Their wings flutter so fast they blur. The wings make buzzing sounds on a summer day.

Brown bees, green bees, big bees, small bees—more than 20,000 kinds of bees buzz on Earth.

4

Bees live everywhere except in water and the planet's coldest places.

Two Kinds of Bees

Most bees live alone. They are called solitary bees. Solitary bees make small nests in dirt or wood. Some use wax from their bodies to make a little room in the nest. This is a cell.

A female solitary bee lays one egg in the cell. She adds some food. Then she closes the cell. A baby bee will grow inside it.

Other bees live in groups. Bees that live together are called social bees. Their group is called a colony.

Fuzzy, striped bumblebees are this kind of bee. They live together in hives. The hives have many wax cells for baby bees.

Life in a Hive

Thousands of bees can live in a social bee colony. Each bee has a special job. Most are workers. They gather food. They take care of the whole colony. These busy bees are all females, but they do not lay eggs. That job is for the queen.

The rest of the bees are males. Their only job is to mate with the queen so she can lay eggs.

worker

A colony can have only one queen. When she is young, she flies out to mate with males. Then she returns to the hive. She stays there, laying eggs.

queen

male

11

A honeybee queen lays pearly white eggs. She puts one egg in each cell. After three days, the egg opens. Out crawls a creature that looks like a small, white worm. It is a larva.

Each wax cell in a honeybee hive has six sides. Some cells are for growing eggs. Some cells store honey. People harvest the honey to eat.

egg

larva

13

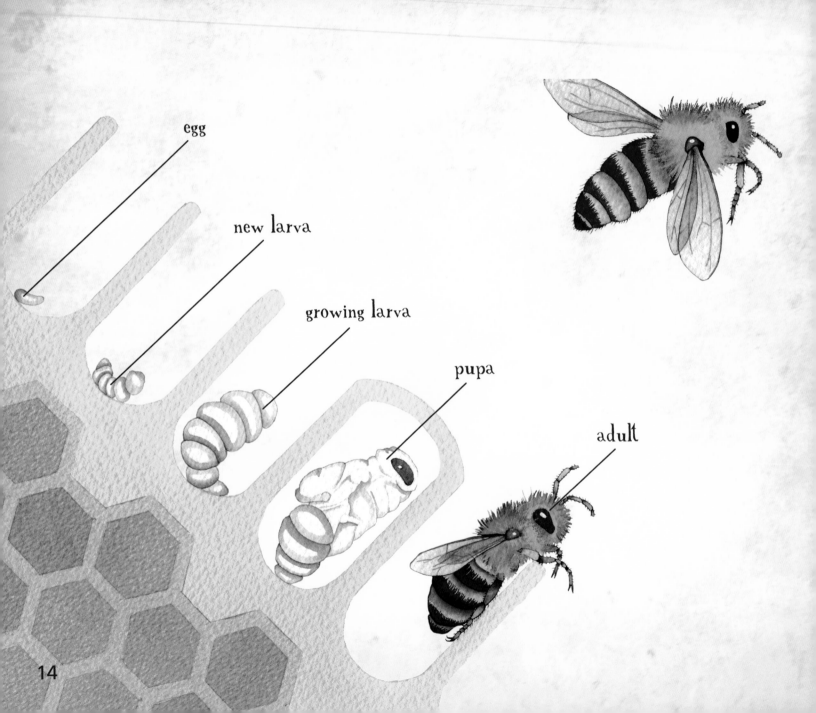

egg

new larva

growing larva

pupa

adult

14

Workers feed the larva. It grows some more. Then, the workers seal off the top of the cell with wax. Inside, the larva begins to change again.

The larva builds a cocoon around its body. It is now a pupa. It continues to grow and change. It becomes an adult bee. Then it bites its way out of the cell.

Finding Food

An adult bee is ready to look for food. It gathers food from flowers. It finds the right flower with the help of its large compound eyes. Honeybees can see colors humans can't. They can tell the shape patterns that make up different flowers.

The bee's antennae wave on its head. The bee uses them to smell and touch.

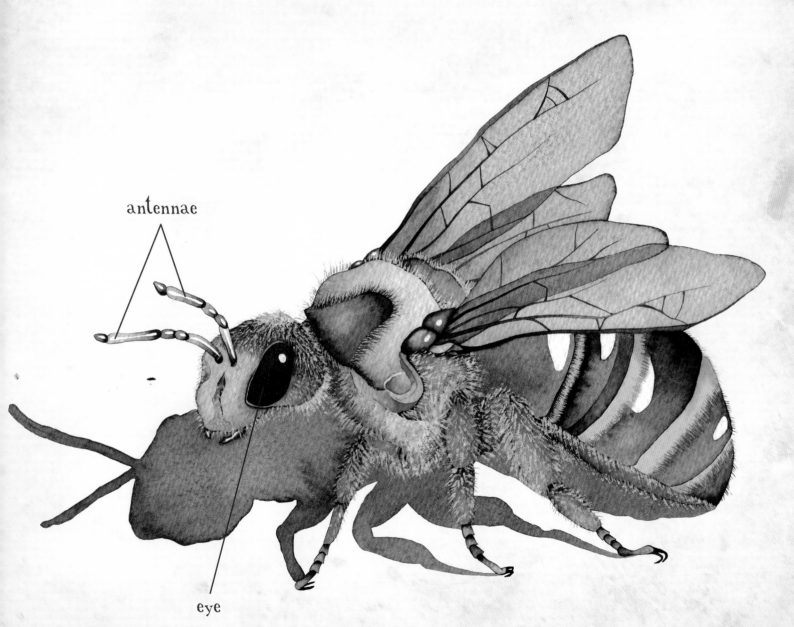

antennae

eye

Buzz, buzz. The bee lands on a flower. It gathers up some of the flower's dusty, yellow pollen in its back legs. A long tube sticks out from the bee's mouth. With the tube, the bee sucks up the flower's sweet nectar.

The bee brings the food back to its nest. The pollen and nectar will feed the baby bees. The nectar may be stored inside a cell. It will turn into honey to feed the colony during the cold, dead winter.

Some bees carry pollen in special spots on their back legs. This spot is called a pollen basket. It is curved like a bowl. It has long, curved hairs along its edges.

Bees need flowers to live, but flowers need bees, too. When a bee visits a flower, pollen sticks to its body. At the next flower, some of that pollen falls off. This helps the flowers make seeds. The seeds make new plants.

In a honeybee colony, scout bees have a special job. These worker bees fly around to find food. Then they come back to the hive. They dance to tell the others where to go.

To dance, the scouts crawl in loops inside the hive. Their bodies trace the number 8. Their dance tells the others which way to go. It shows how far to fly.

Attack!

Many animals eat honey. So do people. Even bees from other colonies will attack a honeybee hive to get its honey.

Workers called guards keep watch over the hive's entrance. They pick out strangers by their smell. Then the bees attack. They push their stingers into their enemy. The bee's body pumps poison into the wound.

A worker honeybee will sting whenever it feels danger. The stinger pulls out of its body during the attack.

stinger

25

The Hive Lives On

Worker bees live just a few weeks or months. But a colony can exist for years and years.

In winter, all the honeybees crowd inside the hive. Their bodies shiver. In this way, the whole hive stays warm.

The queen bee lives between one and five years. When she dies, a new queen takes over. She lays more eggs. New workers hatch. *Buzz, buzz.* In summer, they fly out in search of flowers.

A Bee's Body

A bee's body has three main parts: the head, the thorax, and the abdomen. A bee is protected by a hard casing on the outside of its body.

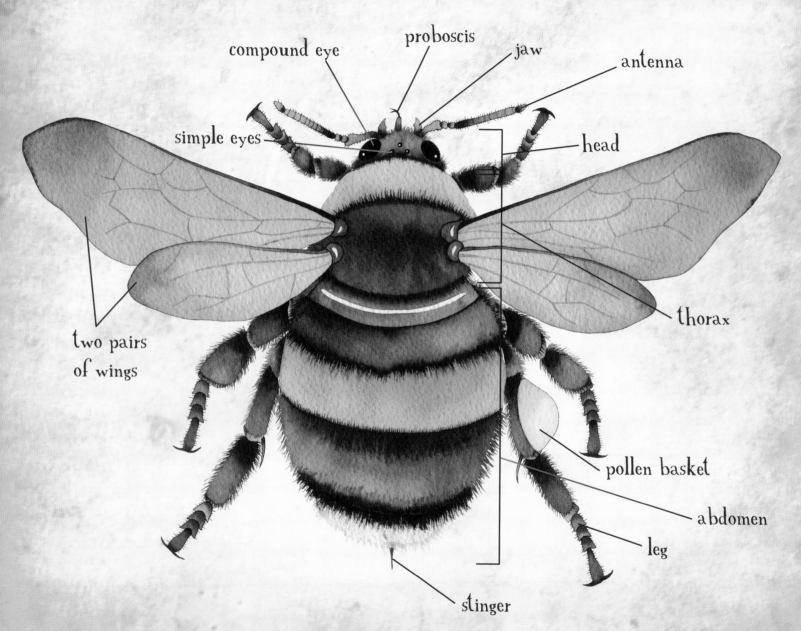

compound eye proboscis jaw

antenna

simple eyes

head

two pairs
of wings

thorax

pollen basket

abdomen

leg

stinger

29

A Closer Look

How a Bee Sees

Bees have two different types of eyes. A simple eye has one lens. A compound eye has many lenses. Find out how a bee sees!

What you need:

- ten drinking straws
- tape
- paper towel tube
- picture of a flower
- notebook paper
- pencil

Hold the straws tightly in your fist. Tap the edges against a table so they are even. Ask a friend to tape the straws around the middle.

Draw a line down the middle of a piece of paper. Title one side "Many" and the other side "One." Look through the straws at the picture of a flower. Write what you see under "Many." Look through the paper towel tube at the picture. Write what you see under "One." How are the views different?

Bee Facts

- A worker honeybee dies after it stings something.
- Worker honeybees move their wings very quickly to keep the hive cool. They act like a fan if the hive is too hot.

Glossary

abdomen—the back part of an insect's body.

antenna (an-**TEH**-nuh)—one of the two long, thin body parts that sticks out from an insect's head and is used to feel and smell.

cocoon—a silk bag a larva spins around itself. Inside the cocoon, the larva changes into an adult insect.

colony—a population of plants or animals in a certain place that belongs to a single species.

compound eye—an eye made up of thousands of lenses, with each one taking in a piece of an image.

pollen—a fine, yellowish powder released from flowers.

social—bugs or animals that live in groups.

solitary—bugs or animals that live alone.

thorax— the middle part of an insect's body.

On the Web

To learn more about bees, visit ABDO Group online at **www.abdopublishing.com**. Web sites about bees are featured on our Book Links page. These links are routinely monitored and updated to provide the most current information available.

Index